# The Women's Rights Movement and Abolitionism

Susan Dudley Gold

Cavendish Square

New York

*Dedicated to my Swirly-Eyed Sister, Jane Hamblen, whose passion for worthwhile causes inspires me.*

*With thanks to Carol Ezell-Gilson of Charleston, South Carolina, whose knowledgeable and informative Grimké Sisters Tour* (http://grimkesisterstour.com) *brought the sisters to life.*

Published in 2016 by Cavendish Square Publishing, LLC
243 5th Avenue, Suite 136, New York, NY 10016

Cataloging-in-Publication Data

Gold, Susan Dudley.
The Women's Rights Movement and abolitionism / by Susan Dudley Gold.
p. cm. — (Primary sources of the abolitionist movement)
Includes index.
ISBN 978-1-50260-536-8 (hardcover) ISBN 978-1-50260-537-5 (ebook)
1. Women's rights — United States — History — 19th century — Juvenile literature.
2. Antislavery movements — United States — Juvenile literature. I. Gold, Susan Dudley. II. Title.
HQ1155.G65 2016
305.42'0973—d23

Editorial Director: David McNamara
Editor: Amy Hayes
Copy Editor: Cynthia Roby
Art Director: Jeffrey Talbot
Senior Designer: Amy Greenan
Senior Production Manager: Jennifer Ryder-Talbot
Production Editor: Renni Johnson
Photo Researcher: J8 Media

# CONTENTS

# What a Woman Can't Do

I magine that you are a woman living in the United States during the 1700s and 1800s. According to law, you are not allowed to vote for president. In fact, in almost all states, you cannot serve on a jury, control the money you inherit or earn, hold professional jobs such as doctor or lawyer, or have any legal control over your children's lives.

If you are a white woman of the upper classes, your family and society expect you to marry, raise children, and oversee household duties. If you do not marry, society dictates that you remain living with relatives and help with household chores. If you are single and choose to work, few jobs are open to you. Some women become teachers, but they receive lower salaries than men. Others work as tutors or help with childcare. A handful of talented women earn money from writing articles or books. Established male writers, however, mock their work and describe them as a "mob of scribbling women."

Upper-class American women living in the 1800s were expected to follow strict rules of behavior and dress. The fancy gowns pictured here were highlighted in *Godey's Lady's Book,* a popular women's magazine, in 1866.

Women, even famous ones, were forbidden to address "mixed" groups of men and women in public. When Harriet Beecher Stowe, author of *Uncle Tom's Cabin,* toured England and the rest of Europe in the 1850s, her brother and husband addressed the crowds waiting to see her.

Most men, and some women, believed that women were the "weaker sex" and could do only certain tasks (considered "women's work," such as raising children and caring for men). They thought women did not have the brains to study or understand complex ideas and had to be "protected" from the disagreeable topics that arose when discussing politics. Such protection meant women could take no role in the wider world beyond their homes and the closed society in which they lived.

The protection of women, however, did not extend to the lower classes or to slave women, both of whom had to work hard to survive. If you were a poor woman, you

Female slaves had to labor alongside male slaves on Southern plantations.

probably worked in a menial job to help support your family. You, too, would have had few rights. Poor women toiled at textile factories, washed laundry, sewed and repaired clothing, or served as maids or housekeepers in the homes of the wealthy. The money they earned went to their husbands. They, like richer women in America, could not serve as guardians of their children, vote, or make key decisions about their own lives.

Slave women had no rights at all. Overseers forced female slaves to work alongside male slaves in the fields, tending crops under a broiling sun or performing other difficult tasks, sometimes in chains to prevent their escape. Both men and women endured savage beatings. Those black women who served as maids, housekeepers, and nannies worked long hours and performed at the mercy of their white masters.

As white women took up the cause of these enslaved black Americans, they began to see that they, too, wore chains. The two causes—freedom from slavery and rights for women—grew together and developed into powerful movements that eventually would free black Americans and make gains toward establishing equal rights for all.

# CHAPTER ONE

# A Cause Worth Dying For

S arah and Angelina Grimké did not fit the profile of crusaders seeking freedom for slaves and equal rights for women. Raised on a slave-owning plantation in South Carolina, they were the proper daughters of a well-respected judge and his wife. The Grimkés were among the elite of Charleston's high society. John Grimké, a justice of South Carolina's Supreme Court, was among the state's most powerful men. His wife, Mary Smith, came from one of the wealthiest families in town. The Grimké family participated in all the events that Charleston's high society had to offer.

The Grimkés owned a large plantation in Beaufort, South Carolina, and an elegant house in Charleston. Hundreds of slaves toiled on their plantation; more slaves

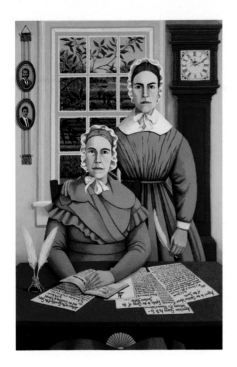

There are few images of Sarah and Angelina Grimké. Carol Ezell-Gilson presents them here in Belleville, the first boarding school the sisters operated in New Jersey. On the writing desk are the sisters' most important papers written in support of abolition and women's rights.

worked in the Charleston house. In South Carolina, as in the rest of the South, only the largest plantations had more than a few slaves. Most farmers relied on a handful of slaves or rented them from wealthier landowners.

As children, both Sarah and Angelina heard the screams of agony from slaves whipped and tortured at the nearby **workhouse**. Guards at the workhouse used whips, chains, and torture devices to punish slaves at their masters' request. In extreme cases, the disembodied head of a dead slave served as a gory warning to other slaves to follow the master's orders without complaint—a gruesome sight Sarah told of seeing as a girl. On the streets of Charleston, slaves went on the auction block not far from their home. Young children sobbed wildly as the auctioneer pulled them away from their parents' arms and sold them to masters on distant plantations. The sisters would have seen the boatloads of slaves being brought to Charleston or shipped to other ports. They would have heard the clink of chains as black men, women, and children trudged along the city's wharves near the Grimké home.

Horrified by such images of slavery, Sarah and Angelina Grimké rejected a life of privilege as wealthy Southern belles. Instead, they would lead the way—first as **abolitionists** and later as women seeking their own rights—for a generation of American women activists.

Southern landowners brought slaves to the workhouse to be punished. Here, a slave hangs from the rafters while an overseer prepares to administer a beating with the lash.

Sarah recognized the cruelty of slavery early in life. When she was only five years old, she witnessed the vicious beating of a slave who labored at the family's house in Charleston. Sickened by the sight, she ran away from home. Her family found her walking on the docks along the waterfront. She had been asking sea captains there to take her to a land where there was no slavery.

At age eleven, Sarah taught Hetty—the young slave girl who was her playmate and who combed her hair and performed other tasks—how to read. When her father found out, he punished both girls severely. The laws of South Carolina made it a crime to teach slaves reading or writing. Judge Grimké had helped pass those laws. Sarah never forgot the incident. It marked the beginning of her personal campaign to end slavery. Years later, she recalled her defiance in the face of such laws:

> I took an almost malicious satisfaction in teaching my little waiting-maid at night, when she was supposed to be occupied in combing and brushing my locks. The light was put out, the key hole screened, and flat on our stomachs before the fire, with the spelling-book under our eyes, we defied the law of South Carolina.

During her childhood, Sarah attended the Episcopal Church in Charleston with her family. She became a committed Christian and taught Sunday school to the slave children owned by the white members of the church. Because of the laws, Sarah could not teach the children to read the Bible themselves; they could only listen to the stories she told them. Sarah thought the restrictions made no sense. She also became convinced, after studying the Bible and seeing the treatment of slaves firsthand, that slavery was a sin.

Seeking a religion that supported her beliefs, Sarah left home and the South and joined the **Quakers** in Philadelphia in 1821. The first Quakers—members of a Christian religion known as the Religious Society of Friends—settled in America in the late 1600s. Some Quakers owned slaves, but by the 1800s the religion had ejected all slave owners from its membership. In 1790, the religious group submitted a petition to Congress to

# Sarah Grimké: Would-Be Lawyer

Sarah Grimké, born in 1792, was an exceptionally bright child. She read her father's law books and longed to pursue studies open only to males. Her older brother Thomas shared his books with her, and she taught herself geography, mathematics, and history. She discussed politics, art and literature, religion, and ideas on other topics with her father and brothers.

Judge Grimké once remarked that Sarah would have been the greatest lawyer in all of South Carolina—had she not been a girl. That became her dream, to follow her brothers and fathers in the practice of law. At the time and for many years to come, the legal profession barred women from becoming lawyers. Not until 1869 would a woman become a lawyer in the United States.

When Sarah's father discovered her studying Latin, he put a stop to her self-taught lessons. Girls, he told her, had no business reading Latin. In the tightly controlled society of early nineteenth-century America, women belonged only in the realm of home—as mother, wife, daughter, or unmarried aunt.

end slavery in the United States.

In the Quaker tradition, unlike mainstream denominations, women spoke out in meetings. Used to expressing their views, several Quaker women became leaders in the fight against slavery. Lucretia Mott, one of the early leaders in the antislavery campaign, was a Quaker minister. She and her husband, James Mott, opened their home in Pennsylvania to runaway slaves and spoke out against slavery. Susan B. Anthony, Abby Kelley Foster, Mary Ann McClintock, Jane Hunt, and Martha Wright— all were Quakers and all dedicated themselves to end slavery and later, to win rights for women. In Philadelphia, Sarah became friendly with the Motts and others of the Quaker faith who opposed slavery.

Many of the Quakers involved in the abolition movement provided secret hiding places for fugitive slaves seeking freedom.

Influenced by her older sister, Angelina, who was thirteen years younger than Sarah, soon adopted the same views about slavery. She once fainted when she saw ugly scars on the back of a young slave boy who worked at her elementary school. Angelina's refusal to be confirmed in the church because she did not agree with the pledge she was required to take caused a huge controversy. Later, Angelina would follow Sarah in joining the Quakers.

As a young woman, Angelina tried to convince her family and others that slavery was sinful and that they should free their slaves. Realizing finally that she could not succeed in changing their minds, Angelina went to live with Sarah in Pennsylvania in 1827.

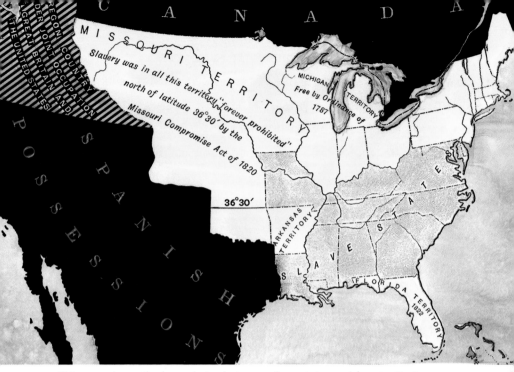

This map shows the boundaries between slave states and free territories determined by the Missouri Compromise of 1820.

## We Will Be Heard

By adopting the Missouri Compromise in 1820, Congress tried to steer a path between the slave owners in the South and antislavery forces in the North. Under the compromise, lawmakers allowed slavery to spread to Missouri but banned it in northern territories. The deal enraged abolitionists, who wanted to end slavery, not expand its reach. They increased their efforts to win converts and abolish slavery.

In 1831, Boston abolitionist William Lloyd Garrison began publishing *The Liberator*. The weekly newspaper became the voice of the antislavery movement. It would later take on the cause of women's rights, seeking equal rights for all—male and female, black and white. In its first issue, published January 1, 1831, Garrison pledged to work for the same rights for the nation's slaves as those promised by the Declaration of Independence: "that all men are created equal, and endowed by their Creator with certain inalienable rights—among which are life, liberty and the pursuit of happiness." In strong words Garrison made it clear that he would do whatever he could to end slavery immediately:

> Tell a man whose house is on fire, to give a moderate alarm; tell him to moderately rescue his wife from the hand of the ravisher; tell the mother to gradually extricate her babe from the fire into which it has fallen;—but urge me not to use moderation in a cause like the present. I am in earnest—I will not equivocate—I will not excuse—I will not retreat a single inch—AND I WILL BE HEARD.

Garrison and his followers formed one of the first antislavery organizations, the New England Anti-Slavery Society, in 1832. In 1833, local societies, including the Massachusetts General Colored Association and other black groups, joined to form the American Anti-Slavery Society (AAS) in Philadelphia. Brothers Arthur and Lewis Tappan, wealthy New York merchants who supported many liberal causes, poured money into the abolition effort. At the helm of the new group, Garrison and the Tappans led dedicated abolitionists in an organized, well-funded effort to end slavery. The society

Lewis Tappan, shown here, and his brother Arthur helped finance the US abolition movement.

sent agents throughout New England to lecture to groups, hold meetings, and recruit supporters.

Theodore Weld became one of the most effective activists in the abolitionist cause. While a student at Lane Theological Seminary in Cincinnati, Ohio, he organized a band of students who agitated for an immediate end to slavery and organized antislavery debates. When the school shut down the debates, Weld left and led an aggressive campaign against slavery in Ohio. As agent in charge of the AAS's movement in Ohio, Weld took on the job of winning over westerners to the abolitionist side. His radical views and passionate antislavery speeches made him the target of mobs. At one point he was known as the most mobbed man in America.

## Never Surrender

Weld was not the only abolitionist to face violence from mobs. The more outspoken abolitionists grew, the more violent those who disagreed with them became. Abolitionists speaking throughout the North encountered many people intent on silencing them. Unruly mobs threw rotten eggs and bricks at speakers.

An anti-abolitionist mob seizes newspaper publisher William Lloyd Garrison in Boston in 1835. The abolition leader narrowly escaped serious injury during the incident.

They attacked abolitionists and destroyed their property. They interrupted meetings and burned antislavery brochures and pamphlets. *The Liberator* reported many of these incidents and denounced officials who put up with, and often encouraged, mob rule. An August 15, 1835, article in *The Liberator* criticized Northern newspapers for inciting mobs. "If any thing will overturn and destroy our government, it is mob-law, set on foot or encouraged by secret societies or secret intrigue," the article noted. That October, Garrison himself would be threatened and nearly killed by an angry mob in Boston. In the face of attacks and intimidation, Garrison preached forgiveness and nonviolence.

In Philadelphia, Angelina Grimké was so moved by *The Liberator*'s reports of brave abolitionists who stood firm against mob violence that she sent Garrison a letter outlining her views. In it, she expressed her gratitude that Garrison and other abolitionists continued their campaign against slavery, despite the attacks. She applauded the righteousness of the fight against slavery:

> The ground upon which you stand is holy ground: never—never surrender it. If you surrender it, the hope of the slave is extinguished, and the chains of his servitude will be strengthened a hundred fold. But let no man take your crown, and success is as certain as the rising of to-morrow's sun …
>
> If persecution is the means which God has ordained for the accomplishment of this great end, EMANCIPATION; then, in dependence upon him for strength to bear it, I feel as if I could say, LET IT COME; for it is my deep, solemn, deliberate conviction, that *this is a cause worth dying for.*

Angelina noted that she based her views on what she had "seen, and heard, and known in a land of slavery."

Garrison wrote in an introduction to the letter that he was "thrilled—subdued—strengthened—sole-animated" when he read Angelina's words. He predicted that the letter would be widely read "with admiration and thanksgiving" by readers in 1835 and by students of the nation's history many years in the future. The letter, which Garrison published in the September 19, 1835 edition of *The Liberator*, rocketed Angelina and Sarah Grimké to fame.

# CHAPTER TWO

# The Grimké Sisters: Leading the Way

**A**ngelina's letter to *The Liberator* caused a sensation among abolitionists. Seeing its power to win support for the cause, Garrison republished it as a flyer, or **broadsheet**, which he distributed widely. Other newspapers reprinted the letter. Soon, Sarah, as well as Angelina, came under the spotlight. They became two of the most famous women of their time—known as the South's antislavery sisters.

In July 1836, Angelina reached out to the women of the South—once her friends and compatriots. Her heartfelt "Appeal to the Christian Women of the South" outlined the case against slavery and urged women to do whatever they could to free the slaves. If they did not, Angelina feared that the nation would face a bitter civil war over the issue. Her prediction—if not her hopes—

Angelina Grimké rejected a life of ease on a Southern plantation and moved North to become a leading voice against slavery.

would eventually come true. Relying on the Bible and the US Constitution, she portrayed slavery as a sin. She maintained that slavery not only disobeyed God's rule, it also violated American ideals.

"The *women of the South can overthrow* this horrible system of oppression and cruelty, licentiousness and wrong," she told her readers. She advised them to read about slavery, to pray, to speak against slavery, and to take action by freeing their own slaves, petitioning their state legislators, and following the example of other "noble women who have been raised up in the church to effect great revolutions." That fall the American Anti-Slavery Society published the appeal as a thirty-six-page pamphlet and sent thousands of copies to the South. Officials destroyed every pamphlet they could find.

Although Angelina had aimed the appeal at Southern women, women in the North applauded its message and embraced her declaration that women had the power to change history.

Sarah followed Angelina's appeal with one of her own, this one directed at Southern ministers. For years Southern ministers had preached that the Bible endorsed slavery. Written in December 1836, "An Epistle to the Clergy of the Southern States" urged religious leaders in the South to take a stand against slavery. Like Angelina's appeal, Sarah's letter was printed and distributed in the North and the South, though Southern officials burned all the copies they found.

The Grimkés' father had died in 1819, but their mother and other family members remained in Charleston. They felt the sting of disapproval from friends and neighbors. Officials warned the family that the "infamous" sisters would not be welcome—and might be in danger—if they returned home to South Carolina. The Quakers in Philadelphia also disapproved of the public stance the Grimkés had taken against slavery. While the Quakers opposed slavery, they did not believe in taking part in politics. Eventually the Grimkés would leave the Quakers because of their disagreement over the issue.

## On the Speakers' Circuit

In 1836, the AAS asked Thomas Weld to recruit and train agents to travel throughout the North and speak out against slavery. Invited to join the class, Sarah and Angelina Grimké became two of the most active agents in the group. They were among the first American women to speak publicly before mixed groups of men and women. The custom of the time prevented women from speaking in public to an audience of men. Only one other

FREEDOM S

EMANCIPATI

THE LIBERATOR

OR COUNTRY IS THE WORLD---OUR COUNTRYMEN ARE ALL MANKIND.

BOSTON, FRIDAY, MARCH 22, 1844.

William Lloyd Garrison's newspaper, *The Liberator*, shown here, served as the voice of the abolition movement in the United States.

woman, Maria Stewart, a free African American from Boston, had spoken publicly to mixed crowds before the Grimkés hit the speakers' circuit. Focusing on abolition and the importance of education in her speeches, Stewart went on to found schools for black students in Baltimore and Washington, DC. Her writings, like those of the Grimkés, found a ready audience in the pages of Garrison's *The Liberator*.

At first, the Grimkés spoke only to small gatherings of women, but their presentations became so popular that they soon had to move to large halls. Both women were talented writers and storytellers. Their descriptions of slavery in the South captured the attention of listeners. The Grimké sisters presented the story of slavery from an entirely new viewpoint—as women whose family owned slaves and who had witnessed its effects not only on the enslaved but also on the enslavers. Their descriptions of slavery, seen during their childhood in South Carolina, made a deep impression on listeners.

Angelina, in particular, spoke with a fire that made her an exceptional orator. Raising her voice to be heard over the mobs outside, she told the audience:

> As a Southerner I feel that it is my duty to stand up here to-night and bear testimony against slavery. I have seen it—I have seen it. I know it has horrors that can never be described. I was brought up under its wing: I witnessed for many years its demoralizing influences, and its destructiveness to human happiness. It is admitted by some that the slave is not happy under the *worst* forms of slavery. But I have *never* seen a happy slave.

Soon men joined the crowds of women attending the Grimkés' speeches. Like Weld, the Grimkés attracted hostile mobs. Their attackers called the sisters sinful and immoral, made outrageous accusations (one particularly vicious rumor implied they wanted to lure black men because they could find no white husbands), referred to Angelina as "Devil-ina," booed their speeches, and threatened them with violence. One newspaper editor in New York went so far as to suggest that women who

# OUTRAGE.

**Fellow Citizens,**

AN

# ABOLITIONIST,

of the most revolting character is among you, exciting the feelings of the North against the South. A seditious Lecture is to be delivered

## THIS EVENING,

at 7 o'clock, at the Presbyterian Church in Cannon-street. You are requested to attend and unite in putting down and silencing by peaceable means this tool of evil and fanaticism. Let the rights of the States guaranteed by the Constitution be protected.

**Feb. 27, 1837.** *The Union forever!*

Broadsheets like the one above publicized abolitionist meetings and incited riots by urging action against antislavery activists, described as the "tool of evil and fanaticism."

traveled around the country for the abolition cause should be "sent to insane asylums."

The Grimkés soldiered on, bringing their message to at least forty thousand people in sixty-seven towns over the course of twenty-three weeks. During that time, they attended eighty-eight meetings and wrote essays that were printed in newspapers and distributed in thousands of pamphlets and flyers.

## Standing Upright

While anti-abolitionists attacked their message, other critics—including church leaders and abolitionists— condemned the Grimkés for speaking in public and filling roles that had been reserved for men only. Congregational ministers in Massachusetts, in their 1837 *Pastoral Letter*, publicly denounced them:

[When a woman] assumes the place and tone of a man as a public reformer, our care and protection of her seem unnecessary, we put ourselves in self defence against her, she yields the power which God has given her for protection, and her character becomes unnatural.

Catharine Beecher, pictured above, led advances in women's education but believed that women had no place in the world of politics.

Catharine Beecher, a noted educator and founder of two schools for girls, wrote that it was "neither appropriate nor wise, nor right" for women to enter the political arena as the Grimkés had done. Men could preach, petition lawmakers, and speak on issues of importance, but women, Beecher claimed, should "win every thing by peace and love." She concluded, "Men are the proper persons to make appeals to the rulers whom they appoint."

The attacks spurred both Sarah and Angelina to assert their right to speak as women and as "moral beings." In July 1837, Sarah Grimké's series, "Letters on the Equality of the Sexes and the Condition of Women," caused a sensation when they were published in the *New England Spectator*, a Boston weekly newspaper. Garrison reprinted the letters in *The Liberator* shortly afterward.

For centuries women had taken a supporting role in reform efforts led by men. Now, Grimké stepped to center stage as an advocate not only for abolition but also for women's rights. In the letters, she laid out a catalogue of wrongs against women—in law, education, business, and religion. She called for women to receive the same pay as men, be given the same rights as other citizens, and receive equal educational opportunities. She disputed claims that God made women inferior and demanded that women be treated as equals:

> All I ask our brethren is, that they will take their feet from off our necks, and permit us to stand upright on that ground which God designed us to occupy.

Sarah censured men for their attempts to "drive women from almost every sphere of moral action." By withholding from women "essential rights," men interfered with women's ability to meet their responsibilities as moral beings, Grimké said. Women, she said, had the same duties as men to take a stand against evil:

> God has made no distinction between men and women as moral beings; … the distinction now so much insisted upon between male and female virtues is as absurd as it is unscriptural … to me it is perfectly clear, that WHATSOEVER IT IS MORALLY RIGHT FOR A MAN TO DO, IT IS MORALLY RIGHT FOR A WOMAN TO DO.

Angelina responded to Beecher's criticisms with her own letter. In it, she, too, defended women's right and duty to work for good causes:

> Human beings have rights, because they are moral beings ... the mere circumstance of sex does not give to man higher rights and responsibilities than to woman.

Angelina noted a truth that other women in the movement would discover as well: that in the course of fighting for the rights of slaves she had come to understand the rights to which she, too, was entitled.

## Women Against Slavery

Despite male resistance, many women took active roles in the campaign to end slavery in the United States. Even without a vote in state and national elections, women could petition Congress, write and publish their views, distribute antislavery flyers, donate money, and speak out, as the Grimkés did, on the outrages of slavery.

At the first convention of the American Anti-Slavery Society in 1833, about one-third of those attending were women. Nevertheless, women and black delegates had no real power. White men held every office, with Lewis Tappan elected as president and Garrison as a secretary in the new organization. Lucretia Mott was among those attending the convention, but neither she nor any of the other women in the hall were allowed to vote. Mott was not asked to sign the declaration passed by the convention, even though the convention adopted several of her suggested revisions to the text. The document, signed by

# "I Will Lift Up My Voice Like a Trumpet"

A crowd of three thousand—assembled for the second Anti-Slavery Convention of American Women—sat spellbound as Angelina Grimké Weld described slavery as she had seen it in her native Charleston. Angelina had married Theodore Weld just two days before, on May 14, 1838. As she spoke, bricks tossed by an angry mob outside crashed through the windows of the newly constructed Pennsylvania Hall. With eyes flashing and cheeks flushed, she asked: "What if the mob should now burst in upon us, break up our meeting, and commit violence upon our persons—would this be any thing compared with what the slaves endure?" Loud roars and sounds of objects being hurled at the building continued, but she kept talking. When the meeting ended, white women linked arms with black women to protect them as they left the building. They dodged stones and insults. The next night, a second mob set fire to the empty building, closed because of safety concerns. Firefighters called to the scene did nothing to put out the flames, and it burned to the ground.

Pennsylvania Hall burns as angry rioters cheer. The Hall was constructed with funds raised in part by women abolitionists.

sixty men, was reproduced in *The Liberator*'s December 14, 1833, issue. In the declaration, the members of the AAS pledged to "secure to the colored population of the United States all the rights and privileges which belong to them as men and as Americans."

Lucretia Mott, a Quaker and leader in the effort to end slavery, helped spearhead the campaign for women's rights.

The fact that the convention ignored the "rights and privileges" of the women in attendance did not go unnoticed by the female members of the group. The women almost immediately formed their own antislavery groups. Lucretia Mott founded one of the first in Philadelphia. Among its members were the Grimké sisters and several leading black abolitionist women in the area. Others sprang up in New York, Boston, and many other cities in the North. By the mid-1830s, women had organized more than one hundred such groups. The groups attracted both black and white women as members.

In May 1837, the regional women's organizations came together to hold the first Antislavery Convention of American Women in New York. It was the first time on record that women had organized a national political convention of that size. Participants included the leading women abolitionists of the time: Lucretia Mott, Abby Kelley Foster (who like the Grimkés was an

Lydia Maria Child wrote extensively about equal rights for Native Americans, slaves, and women.

outstanding public speaker for the abolition cause), Lydia Maria Child (a noted author who challenged white male rule in her writings), Grace Douglass (a black Quaker and one of the founding members of the Philadelphia women's antislavery group), Angelina and Sarah Grimké, and many others who had been in the forefront of the battle against slavery. Seventy-one delegates and 103 "corresponding members" attended. Mott opened the proceedings, and the group elected Mary S. Parker, head of Boston's Female Anti-Slavery Society, as president. Mott and Sarah Grimké were among six vice presidents chosen to serve the organization; Angelina Grimké and three others also served on the executive board.

For four days the women discussed the issues and resolved to take action. Angelina Grimké wasted no time in challenging society's treatment of women. Determined to give women the power to change things, she proposed a resolution:

> [T]he time has come for woman to move in that sphere which Providence has assigned her, and no longer remain satisfied in the circumscribed limits with which corrupt custom and a perverted application of

Scripture have encircled her; therefore that it is the duty of woman, and the province of woman, to plead the cause of the oppressed in our land, and to do all that she can by her voice, and her pen, and her purse, and the influence of her example, to overthrow the horrible system of American slavery.

The resolution was one among many brought forth by the Grimkés. It passed, but not without spirited debate among the delegates. A number of women requested that their names be printed in the proceedings as having opposed the measure.

On February 21, 1838, Angelina broke new ground when she became the first woman in America to testify before a state legislature. Before a packed Massachusetts state house, Grimké presented a petition against slavery signed by twenty thousand women. She spoke on the evils of slavery for more than six hours over three days. Angelina used the opportunity to claim the right, as a woman, to have a say in government. She told the lawmakers: "We are citizens of this republic and as such our honor, happiness, and well-being are bound up in its politics, government, and laws."

Ill health, domestic duties, and money woes kept the Grimkés from active reform efforts much beyond 1839. The views Sarah and Angelina Grimké expressed in the 1830s, however, reached far ahead of their time. Other women would heed their words and build a movement based on the Grimkés' vision of equality between men and women.

# CHAPTER THREE

# A Matter
of Rights

William Lloyd Garrison and Frederick Douglass, an escaped slave who became a leader in the abolition campaign, championed women's rights and women's abilities to fight for the abolitionist cause. Other male abolitionists resisted Garrison's advice not to "overlook" the power of women to further the cause. Some of these men, because of their religious beliefs, thought women were not suited and not meant to participate in the political arena. Others did not want to divert attention and energies to women's rights. They believed that all efforts should be focused on ending slavery.

This difference of opinion about the role of women came to a head at the sixth annual meeting of the American Anti-Slavery Society in 1839. After much debate, the society passed a resolution allowing women to become full members of the society, with the right to vote, speak, and hold office. Three women—Lydia Maria Child, Maria Weston Chapman, and Lucretia Mott—won election to the AAS executive committee. An enraged Lewis Tappan protested, "To put a woman on the committee with men is contrary to the usages of civilized society."

At the AAS meeting the following year, Abby Kelley Foster's nomination to the society's business committee caused another uproar. When she won the election by more than one hundred votes, Lewis Tappan resigned from the committee and with his brother withdrew from the society altogether. Later that year the Tappans and their followers formed a competing national antislavery organization, the American and Foreign Anti-Slavery Society, which barred women from membership.

## No Women Allowed

At the 1840 meeting, AAS members appointed a delegation of men and women to attend the upcoming World Anti-Slavery Convention in London. The organizers of the convention had invited members of antislavery groups around the world to attend the first international convention of abolitionists. Eight American women made the long ocean voyage across the Atlantic to attend the prestigious convention. Lucretia Mott, Sarah Pugh, Abby Kimber, Elizabeth Neall, and Mary Grew represented the Philadelphia and Pennsylvania antislavery groups, while Emily Winslow, Abby Southwick, and

# No Rights for Women or Slaves

The men who founded America did not extend equal rights to women or to black people of either sex. John Adams dismissed his wife Abigail's pleas to "remember the ladies" when forming the new nation's government. Adams, the nation's first vice president and its second president, wrote: "Depend on it, we know better than to repeal our Masculine systems."

Thomas Jefferson, author of the Declaration of Independence and the fourth president of the United States, put women, babies, and slaves in the same category when it came to rights. He wrote in an 1816 letter:

> Were our State a pure democracy, in which all its inhabitants should meet together to transact all their business, there would yet be excluded from their deliberations,
> 1. Infants, until arrived at years of discretion.
> 2. Women, who, to prevent depravation of morals and ambiguity of issue, could not mix promiscuously in the public meetings of men.
> 3. Slaves, from whom the unfortunate state of things with us takes away the rights of will and of property.

Ann Greene Phillips were delegates from Massachusetts. Phillips's husband, the eloquent abolitionist orator Wendell Phillips, also attended. In addition, recently married Elizabeth Cady Stanton accompanied her

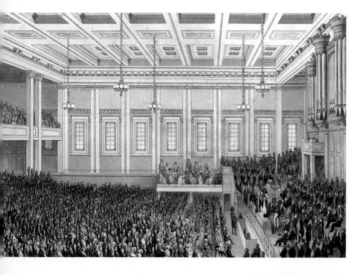

Delegates meet in 1840 in Exeter Hall to join forces in the fight to end slavery. Female delegates from the United States, barred from participating in the proceedings, sit in a gallery separated from the main hall.

husband, Henry Stanton, who went as a delegate of the American and Foreign Anti-Slavery Society.

On June 12, 1840, the Americans joined other delegates from around the world who had walked through London's narrow cobblestone streets to the magnificent Exeter Hall. Former slaves joined Londoners; Scottish ministers walked with men from Jamaica, Sierra Leone, Paris, and New York City—all gathered with the one goal of eliminating slavery from the face of the earth. In addition to the five hundred delegates, a thousand spectators crowded into the grand hall and spilled into the street outside.

An unpleasant surprise awaited the female delegates from America. When the women, many in modest Quaker dresses, entered the hall, their English hosts blocked their way. In a calm but firm voice, Mott insisted that the women be admitted and that the convention as a whole determine their status as delegates. The participants argued for more than an hour on whether to seat the women. Massachusetts delegate Wendell Phillips made a motion that the women be accepted as full delegates:

> [W]e do not think it just or equitable ... that after the trouble, the sacrifice, the self-devotion of a part of those who leave their families, and kindred, and occupations in their own land, to come 4,000 miles to attend this World's Convention, they should be refused a place in its deliberations.

Wendell Phillips spoke eloquently in favor of allowing women to take part in the international convention to end slavery.

Several others strongly objected to the move to ban the women. Harvard Professor William Adam, a noted Massachusetts abolitionist, told the gathering that if the women were not considered qualified to be delegates, then he would not be a qualified delegate either. "I have no other authority to appear amongst you," he told the convention, "to take place in your proceedings, and give a voice in your deliberations, than that right which is equally possessed by the ladies to whom a place among you has been denied." He added that efforts by American women for the abolition cause was "the very life of us, and of all that we have done, and all we hope to do."

Opponents acknowledged the women's contributions but vehemently objected to their participation at the convention. At one point several English ministers waved Bibles in the faces of those who favored the women's position.

Finally, the convention voted by an "overwhelming majority" to bar women as delegates. The women remained in the hall but were assigned seats in a small gallery with a curtain separating them from the main floor. They were not allowed to address the gathering or express their views.

William Lloyd Garrison, arriving after the vote was taken, refused to be seated as a delegate unless the entire AAS delegation was admitted. For the remainder of the sessions, he, Adam, and other supporters sat in the small gallery with the women. Garrison would later declare:

> I have been derisively called a "Woman Rights Man." I know no such distinction. I claim to be a HUMAN RIGHTS Man; and wherever there is a human being, I see God-given rights inherent in that being, whatever may be the sex or complexion.

The American women were not pleased with their treatment at the convention. As Lucretia Mott and Elizabeth Cady Stanton walked arm in arm along the London streets to their hotel after the day's proceedings, they resolved then and there to hold their own convention—on women's rights—once they returned home. The two women concluded that men at the convention had a "great need of some education on that question."

With Lucretia Mott and three other women, Elizabeth Cady Stanton organized the first women's rights convention in Seneca Falls, New York. Stanton was a leading figure in the decades-long battle to win equal rights and the vote for women.

## A Declaration of Rights and Sentiments

On Thursday, July 13, 1848, Stanton and Mott, along with Mott's sister Martha C. Wright and Mary Ann McClintock, met in the home of Jane and Richard Hunt in Waterloo, New York. The women gathered around the table had much in common. All five were married and had children, all but Stanton had been raised as Quakers, and most were active in the abolition movement. All believed that women should be treated as the equals of men.

The best course of action, they decided, would be to call a meeting to discuss women's rights. A local minister agreed to let the women hold the event in the Wesleyan Methodist Chapel in nearby Seneca Falls. That afternoon they composed a notice to advertise the meeting, which they scheduled for July 19 and 20. The next day, the *Seneca County Courier* carried an announcement of the meeting:

> **Woman's Rights Convention:**
> A Convention to discuss the Social, Civil and Religious Condition and Rights of Woman, will be held in the Wesleyan Chapel at Seneca Falls, New York, on

Wednesday and Thursday, the 19th and
20th of July instant. During the first day,
the meetings will be exclusively for women,
which all are earnestly invited to attend. The
public generally are invited to be present
on the second day, when Lucretia Mott, of
Philadelphia, and others, both ladies and
gentlemen, will address the Convention.

On Sunday the women met again to plan the
convention, which was to take place in three days. Using
the Declaration of Independence as a guide, they crafted
"A Declaration of Rights and Sentiments." Stanton wrote
the final version, which made slight—but important—
changes to the US Declaration. It included the passage:

We hold these truths to be self-evident:
that all men and women are created equal;
that they are endowed by their Creator with
certain inalienable rights; that among these
are life, liberty, and the pursuit of happiness;
that to secure these rights governments are
instituted, deriving their just powers from
the consent of the governed.

Among the grievances listed in the document,
Stanton addressed lower pay for women, unfair divorce
and custody laws, and the barring of women from many
professions, institutes of higher learning, and leadership
roles in churches. Eleven resolutions accompanied
the declaration. These called for equality for women,
supported the right and duty of women to work for

Pamphlets like the one shown at left publicized the Declaration of Sentiments, resolutions, and other details of the Seneca Falls women's rights convention.

reform, and stated the right of women to speak in public and hold public office. The most controversial called for the right of women to vote. British women called themselves suffragettes from the word **suffrage**, meaning the right to vote. American women who lobbied for the vote became known as **suffragists**.

With the exception of Mott, none of the women had experience in organizing or running meetings. They called on James Mott, Lucretia's husband, to serve as chairman of the convention. On the morning of the event, the women arrived at the church to find crowds of people waiting and the chapel's door locked. A young male relative climbed through a window and unlatched the lock. Men and women, eager to witness the proceedings, filled the church. Originally the organizers had planned to open the first day's proceedings to women only, but they decided to let the men remain.

During the first day's session, Stanton read the declaration, and the convention reviewed it, paragraph

The waterwall at the Women's Rights National Historical Park in Seneca Falls exhibits the text and signers of the Declaration of Sentiments.

by paragraph. One hundred people, sixty-eight women and thirty-two men, signed the declaration, including Frederick Douglass and the husbands of Mott, Hunt, and McClintock. More debate revolved around the resolutions. Some believed asking for the vote would put the entire campaign for equal rights at risk. But Stanton and Douglass both spoke passionately on the right to vote. The convention closed by approving all the resolutions with a large majority. Lucretia Mott ended the meeting with a rousing appeal to continue the campaign for women's rights.

The event made news throughout the region. Some applauded the women's convention and their campaign. Garrison published a report of the proceedings in the August 25 edition of *The Liberator*. A brief article in the paper's September 1 edition titled "Woman's Revolution" noted that the convention had "aimed a blow ... that will be effective in assigning to Woman her just position in society."

In the *North Star*, Douglass described the Declaration of Sentiments as "the basis of a grand movement." He gave strong support to the cause of women's rights:

> [I]f that government only is just which governs by the free consent of the governed, there can be no reason in the world for denying to woman the exercise of the [vote], or a hand in making and administering the laws of the land.

Many more newspapers ridiculed the convention and attacked those who attended. One anonymous critic described the organizers as "erratic" and "addle-pated" and the proceedings as "a most insane and ludicrous farce." Harsher critics portrayed the women as godless radicals or amazons who neglected their family duties. The *Oneida Whig* stated that the convention was "the most shocking and unnatural incident ever recorded in the history of womanity." Ministers preached from their pulpits that equal rights would degrade women. The abuse became so intense that some of those who signed the declaration withdrew their names.

Nevertheless, the convention had far-reaching results in the struggle for women's rights. Stanton later wrote of the Seneca Falls meeting, "the brave protests sent out from this Convention touched a responsive chord in the hearts of women all over the country." Trained in the trenches of the abolition campaign, women had finally taken up the cause of equal rights on their own behalf.

# Rights
# for All

The landmark convention at Seneca Falls lit a fire that would spread to women throughout the nation. Men joined the effort as well. Two weeks after the Seneca Falls meeting, women in Rochester, New York, held another convention to add their names to the Declaration of Rights and Sentiments and explore women's rights further. Amy Post, a Quaker who had attended the Seneca Falls convention, and others organized the event. In a bold move, the committee asked a woman, Abigail Bush, to preside over the meeting. Elizabeth Cady Stanton and Lucretia Mott questioned the wisdom of having a woman chair the proceedings, but

Lucy Stone, pictured here, spoke out against slavery and helped organize the first national women's rights convention.

Bush's capable handling of the meeting quelled their doubts. Stanton later apologized to Post for her initial opposition to the idea. More than one hundred new supporters signed the declaration after Stanton read it to the gathering.

The next women's rights meeting, in April 1850, convened in Salem, Ohio. As at the other conventions, participants committed themselves to the declaration of Seneca Falls and called for the right to vote. To further their cause, women petitioned state and national lawmakers to pass legislation supporting women's rights. Stanton and others wrote articles and editorials on the topic.

In spring of 1850, the American Anti-Slavery Convention, held in Boston, served as a launch site for a national women's rights event. At the end of the antislavery meeting, William Lloyd Garrison suggested that those interested in women's rights hold a national convention. Nine women answered the call, including Lucy Stone, Abby Kelley Foster, Harriot Kezia Hunt, and Paulina Wright Davis. Stone had recently graduated from Oberlin College, the first woman in Massachusetts to earn a bachelor's degree. Like Foster, she worked as an agent for the AAS, speaking to audiences about women's rights as well as abolition. Davis, a lecturer and wealthy supporter of abolition, later launched a magazine devoted to the "elevation of women." Hunt, one of the first American women to work professionally as a doctor, was particularly interested in the medical education of women.

These women organized the first national women's rights convention in the United States, held in Worcester, Massachusetts, on October 23 and 24, 1850. The convention attracted more than one thousand people. Delegates came from almost all the Northern states and included women and men, blacks and whites. Stanton sent a letter of support, but she was pregnant with her fourth child and did not attend. Davis presided over the convention and gave the opening remarks. Mott, Abby Price (a poet and lecturer on women's rights), Wendell Phillips, and William Channing (a leading Unitarian minister and abolitionist) all addressed the convention. Sojourner Truth, a former slave whose powerful abolition speeches captivated audiences,

Sojourner Truth, above, a former slave and vibrant speaker, moved audiences with her passionate appeals for equal rights.

also addressed the gathering. Her speech was the first by a black woman at a women's rights convention.

The convention passed, among others, a resolution that all women and men regardless of color had the same rights as white men in America. These rights, the resolutions made clear, applied equally to black men and women, including slaves. Among the delegates who fashioned the resolutions were William Lloyd Garrison, Lucretia Mott, Frederick Douglass, Lucy Stone, and other radical abolitionists who supported equal rights for all.

Some white advocates of women's rights argued against mentioning race—either because they feared it would distract from the issue or because they did not support equal rights for blacks. The issue of race would play a larger role in the push for women's rights after the Civil War.

As at Seneca Falls, the press insulted those attending the Worcester convention and attacked their message. A report in the *New York Herald* described the convention as "that motley mingling of abolitionists, socialists, and infidels, of all sexes and colors."

Organizers held a second national women's rights convention in Worcester in 1851. Women would continue the annual meeting until the Civil War. By then agents had traveled throughout the North and Midwest to speak for the cause. Women's groups distributed pamphlets, petitioned lawmakers, and lobbied ministers and the press for support. Local and state conventions helped attract women in regions beyond New England, New York, and Pennsylvania. At a convention in Akron, Ohio, in 1851, Sojourner Truth won recognition for her stirring speech:

> That man over there says that women
> need to be helped into carriages, and lifted

over ditches, and to have the best place everywhere. Nobody ever helps me into carriages, or over mud-puddles, or gives me any best place! And ain't I a woman? Look at me! Look at my arm! I have ploughed and planted, and gathered into barns, and no man could head me! And ain't I a woman? …
If the first woman God ever made was strong enough to turn the world upside down all alone, these women together ought to be able to turn it back, and get it right side up again! And now they is asking to do it, the men better let them.

Historians disagree over whether the speech is exactly as Truth said it. Some phrases may have been revised or added by Frances Dana Barker Gage, who presided over the meeting and later printed Truth's words. Regardless of the exact words spoken, the speech echoed through history, inspiring many generations of women and men in the cause of women's rights. For her part, Gage became a leader in the women's rights campaign. She wrote and lectured on the rights of blacks and women throughout the Midwest.

During the 1850s, Mott continued to lead women's rights efforts with the help of Lucy Stone, Susan B. Anthony, Abby Price, and many others. For most of that time, Stanton stayed home with her children—the seventh was born in 1859. At Anthony's urging, she wrote pamphlets, speeches, and essays on women's rights.

# Fighting Sexism with Laughter

**W**omen reformers had to endure the taunts and insults of those who believed a woman's place was in the home and politics was for men only. Talented women like Maria Weston Chapman used poetry and humor to defuse the critics. Chapman wrote "Times to Try Men's Souls" in 1837 after Massachusetts ministers issued their *Pastoral Letter* criticizing the Grimké sisters for speaking out against abolition. The poem made the rounds of the women's rights conventions, lightening the mood and bringing smiles to the listeners:

**Times to Try Men's Souls**

Confusion has seized us, and all things go wrong,
The women have leaped from "their spheres,"
And instead of fixed stars, shoot as comets along,
And are setting the world by the ears! …

They've taken a notion to speak for themselves,
And are wielding the tongue and the pen;
They've mounted the rostrum; the **termagant** elves,
And—oh horrid!—are talking to men! …

Now, misses may reason, and think, and debate,
Til unquestioned submission is quite out of date.
(signed) The Lords of Creation

Suffragist Florence Jaffray "Daisy" Harriman raises a banner with the slogan "Failure Is Impossible" to win support for the Susan B. Anthony Amendment guaranteeing women the right to vote. It took more than forty years for the amendment to be enacted.

Anthony first met her mentor, Stanton, in 1851 when she traveled to Seneca Falls to attend a temperance meeting. Many of the early suffragists also participated in the **temperance movement**, the campaign to ban alcohol. At a meeting of the Sons of Temperance in 1852, the male moderator told Anthony to sit down after she rose to offer a resolution. "The sisters were not invited here to speak, but to listen and learn!" he told a fuming Anthony. She and Stanton left the meeting in a rage. They later became leaders in the Woman's New York State Temperance Society and became partners in the fight for women's equality.

In 1860 the two women played a major role in winning the passage of a New York law that benefited married women. In an impassioned speech before the state legislature, Stanton compared the legal standing of women in the state to that of a slave. Anthony lobbied the lawmakers. Swayed by the women's arguments, the legislature approved the measure. The new law gave married women in New York the right to own property, work and have control over their earnings, sue and be sued, inherit money and property, and have joint custody of their children. Other states would follow suit, though some would take years to adopt similar laws.

The start of the Civil War in 1861 put an end to the yearly women's conventions and slowed efforts for women's rights. During the war and its aftermath, many women devoted their energies to help end slavery and ensure the rights of former slaves. In 1863 Stanton and Anthony founded the Women's Loyal National League. Its five thousand members collected four hundred thousand signatures on petitions urging Congress to free America's slaves. At the time it was the largest petition drive submitted to Congress and helped win support for the cause. The Thirteenth Amendment—passed in 1865 and ratified by the states later that year—ended slavery in the United States. Abraham Lincoln's **Emancipation Proclamation**, issued in 1863, had freed only slaves in Confederate states.

With that victory won, women rededicated themselves to winning voting rights for themselves as well as for black Americans. In 1866, Stone, Stanton, Anthony, and Douglass founded the American Equal Rights Association (AERA).

Civil War soldiers from the North and the South are shown here at the Battle of Chattanooga, an 1863 Union victory that helped turn the course of the war. The North's ultimate victory in the Civil War brought an end to slavery in the United States.

Lucretia Mott served as the organization's first president. Its mission was to "secure Equal Rights to all American citizens, especially the right of suffrage, irrespective of race, color or sex."

After the Civil War, the federal government set up new policies that allowed the Southern states to rejoin the union. Known as the **Reconstruction Era,** this period also marked African Americans' passage from slaves to free citizens. As part of that effort, Congress passed the **Fourteenth** and **Fifteenth Amendments**—which established African Americans as US citizens and barred states from preventing *males* from voting because of their

The Women's Rights Movement and Abolitionism

race. The Fifteenth Amendment specifically declared that the right to vote "shall not be denied or abridged … on account of race, color, or previous condition of servitude." It made no mention of gender.

The omission enraged suffragists, many of whom had battled long and hard to gain the vote for African Americans. Nevertheless, some of those pushing for women's rights continued to work for the amendment. It became clear that the white men in charge of Congress would not support an amendment that opened the ballot box to both women and blacks. Supporters did not want to risk losing the fight for black rights. Frederick Douglass led the effort, though he, too, favored granting the vote to women as well as blacks. Another faction of the women's rights movement, headed by Anthony and Stanton, withdrew support for the amendment. They viewed the amendment as a betrayal by the black community.

The controversy over the passage of the Fourteenth and Fifteenth Amendments temporarily derailed women's campaign for the vote and split the suffragist movement. Anthony and Stanton formed the all-female National Woman Suffrage Association, which campaigned for an amendment granting women the right to vote. Lucy Stone, Douglass, and others formed the American Woman Suffrage Association, which focused on efforts to win voting rights within the states. The two organizations would join forces in 1890 as the National American Woman Suffrage Association. Six years later a group of well-known black civil rights activists, including Harriet Tubman, poet Frances E. W. Harper, journalist Ida B. Wells-Barnett, educator Margaret Murray Washington, newspaper publisher Josephine St. Pierre Ruffin, and writer Mary Church Terrell formed the National Association of Colored Women in Washington, DC. The group worked to further civil rights for blacks and to obtain the vote for women.

In 1888, on the fortieth anniversary of the Seneca Falls convention, Douglass predicted that the battle for women's rights would eventually be won:

Frederick Douglass, a famed abolition leader, supported efforts to win equal rights for blacks and women.

When a great truth once gets abroad in the world, no power on earth can imprison it, or prescribe its limits, or suppress it. It is bound to go on till it becomes the thought of the world. Such a truth is woman's right to equal liberty with man.

Douglass's words would prove true, but it would be for a new generation of women to run the final race toward victory. Congress first considered the **Nineteenth Amendment** (named in honor of Susan B. Anthony) in 1878 and for each session over the next forty-one years. The amendment finally passed in 1919. It became law in 1920 when the Tennessee legislature, by a four-vote margin, became the thirty-sixth

Suffragist leader Alice Paul, standing in front of the suffrage flag, raises a toast to celebrate the ratification of the Nineteenth Amendment guaranteeing women the right to vote.

state to ratify the document. By then, only one of the women who signed the declaration at Seneca Falls—Charlotte Woodward—still lived, and she was too ill to cast her ballot. But for the millions of women who voted in 1920, being able to cast their ballots for US president for the first time marked a turning point in history. Alice Paul, national chair of the Woman's Party, told reporters the day of the historic vote, "Election Day clinches women's right to a voice in Government and marks the final triumph of the suffrage cause."

# Chronology

Dates in green pertain to events discussed in this volume.

**1619** The African slave trade begins in North America.

**1789** US Constitution goes into effect.

**1777–1804** Slavery is abolished in the northern states.

**1808** The foreign slave trade is abolished by Great Britain and the US.

**1833** American Anti-Slavery Society is founded in Philadelphia. Women, including Lucretia Mott, Lucy Stone, and Sarah and Angelina Grimké, take a leading role in the organization.

**1837–1839** The Grimké sisters speak against slavery to overflow audiences in New York and New England.

**1840** The Tappans and their supporters withdraw from the American Anti-Slavery Society and form the American and Foreign Anti-Slavery Society, which bars female members.

**1848** First Women's Rights Convention held in Seneca Falls, New York. Three hundred delegates sign the Declaration of Rights and Sentiments demanding equal rights for women.

**1849** Harriet Tubman escapes from slavery into Pennsylvania.

**1850** US Congress passes the Fugitive Slave Act.

**1851** *Uncle Tom's Cabin* runs as a serial in the abolitionist newspaper *National Era* in Washington, DC.

**1852** Stowe's complete novel, *Uncle Tom's Cabin*, sells millions of copies.

**1854** Congress approves the Kansas-Nebraska Act.

**1855–1860** Harriet Tubman rescues freedom seekers and leads them from Maryland to Canada.

**1856** Proslavery activists attack the antislavery town of Lawrence, Kansas; John Brown leads a raid on a proslavery family, which launches a three-month conflict known as "Bleeding Kansas."

**1857** Supreme Court hands down decision in the *Dred Scott v Sanford* case.

**1859** John Brown launches an attack at Harpers Ferry.

**1860** Abraham Lincoln is elected president; South Carolina secedes from the Union.

**1861**  Civil War begins.

**1863**  Lincoln's Emancipation Proclamation frees the slaves in Confederate-held territory.

**1865**  The Civil War ends. President Lincoln is assassinated. The Thirteenth Amendment to the US Constitution abolishes slavery.

**1866**  The American Equal Rights Association is formed, led by Susan B. Anthony, Elizabeth Cady Stanton, and Frederick Douglass. Its goals are to establish equal rights and the vote for women and African Americans.

**1868**  Fourteenth Amendment grants US citizenship to former slaves.

**1870**  Fifteenth Amendment gives black men the right to vote. The amendment's omission of women's voting rights creates a bitter divide in the women's rights movement. Sarah and Angelina Grimké, Sojourner Truth, and other women are turned away from polls when they attempt to vote.

**1896**  A group of black civil rights activists, incuding Harriet Tubman, form the National Association of Colored Women in Washington, DC. The group works to further civil rights for blacks and obtain the vote for women.

**1920**  The Nineteenth Amendment is ratified by thirty-six states and becomes part of the US Constitution, fourteen years after the death of Susan B. Anthony, for whom the legislation is named.

# Glossary

**abolitionist**  Someone who works to end slavery.

**broadsheet**  A large flyer used to advertise meetings or stir up support or opposition for various causes.

**Emancipation Proclamation**  President Abraham Lincoln's order, in 1863, to free the slaves in the eleven states of the Confederacy.

**Fifteenth Amendment**  An amendment to the US Constitution, ratified in 1870, protecting the right of black men (but not women) to vote.

**Fourteenth Amendment**  An amendment to the US Constitution that, among other things, guarantees citizenship to anyone born in the United States regardless of race. Ratified in 1868.

**Nineteenth Amendment**  An amendment to the US Constitution, ratified in 1920, granting women the right to vote.

**Quaker**  A member of the Religious Society of Friends. Members practiced nonviolent methods to resolve controversies.

**Reconstruction Era** Post Civil War period dedicated to giving former slaves rights and reorganizing and rebuilding the South.

**suffrage** The right to vote in political elections.

**suffragist** A person actively working for the right of women to vote.

**temperance movement** The campaign to ban alcohol.

**termagant** An overbearing or nagging woman; shrew-like.

**workhouse** The building where slave owners took slaves to be punished. Slaves were whipped and tortured on a stretching device.

# Further Information

**Books**

Colman, Penny. *Elizabeth Cady Stanton and Susan B. Anthony: A Friendship That Changed the World.* New York: Henry Holt and Company, 2011.

Kidd, Sue Monk. *The Invention of Wings.* New York: Viking, 2014.

Mosley, Shelley, and John Charles. *The Suffragists in Literature for Youth: The Fight For the Vote.* Literature for Youth Series. Lanham, MD: Scarecrow Press, 2006.

Mountjoy, Shane. *The Women's Rights Movement: Moving Toward Equality.* Reform Movements in American History. New York: Chelsea House Publications, 2007.

Walton, Mary. *A Woman's Crusade: Alice Paul and the Battle for the Ballot.* New York: Palgrave Macmillan Trade, 2010.

## Video

*One Woman, One Vote.* Directed by Ruth Pollak. 2006.
New York: Public Broadcasting System. DVD.

## Websites

**Digital History**

www.digitalhistory.uh.edu

Set up by the College of Education at the University of
Houston, this site offers primary sources on a wide range
of topics related to American history.

**The Liberator**

fair-use.org/the-liberator

Issues of William Lloyd Garrison's newspaper, available
courtesy the Fair Use Repository.

**Primary Documents in History**

www.loc.gov/rr/program/bib/ourdocs/index.html

The Library of Congress's archive of primary documents
related to national historical events.

# Bibliography

All websites accessed March 2, 2015.

Berkin, Carol. *Angelina and Sarah Grimké: Abolitionist Sisters*. Gilder Lehrman Institute of American History. www.gilderlehrman.org.

Brown, Ira V. "'Am I Not a Woman and a Sister?': The Anti-Slavery Conventions of American Women, 1837–1839," *Pennsylvania History* 50 (1983): 1–19.

Cook, Lisa Connelly. *The Radical Egalitarian Agenda of the First National Woman's Rights Convention of 1850*. Worcester Women's History Project. www.wwhp.org/Resources/WomansRights/LisaConnellyCook.pdf

Digital History. www.digitalhistory.uh.edu.

Garrison, William Lloyd. *The Liberator*, 1831–1865. http://fair-use.org/the-liberator.

Grimké, Sarah. *An Epistle to the Clergy of the Southern States*. Antislavery Literature Project. http://antislavery.eserver.org/religious/grimkeepistle/grimkeepistle.html.

———. *Letters on the Equality of the Sexes and the Condition of Women*. Boston: Isaac Knapp, 1838. https://archive.org/details/lettersonequalit00grimrich.

General Association of Massachusetts. "Pastoral Letter." *American Rhetorical Discourse*. 2nd ed. Ed. Ronald F. Reid. Prospect Heights, IL: Waveland Press, 1995. http://users.wfu.edu/zulick/340/pastoralletter.html.

Griffith, Elisabeth. *In Her Own Right: The Life of Elizabeth Cady Stanton*. New York: Oxford University Press, 1984.

National Park Service. "Women's Rights National Historical Park, New York. www.nps.gov/wori/index.htm

Perry, Mark. *Lift Up Thy Voice: The Sarah and Angelina Grimké Family's Journey from Slaveholders to Civil Rights Leaders*. New York: Penguin Books, 2002.

"Primary Documents in History." www.loc.gov/rr/program/bib/ourdocs/index.html

Public Broadcasting System. "Africans in America," www.pbs.org/wgbh/aia/; "Slavery and the Making of America," www.pbs.org/wnet/slavery/.

Rugoff, Milton. *The Beechers: An American Family in the Nineteenth Century*. New York: Harper & Row, 1981.

Stanton, Elizabeth Cady; Susan B. Anthony, and Matilda Joselyn Gage, eds. *History of Woman Suffrage*, Vol. 1. New York: Fowler and Wells, 1881.

Truth, Sojourner. *Ain't I a Woman?* Internet Modern History Sourcebook, Fordham University. http://legacy.fordham.edu/halsall/mod/sojtruth-woman.asp.

Weld, Angelina Grimké. *Appeal to Christian Women of the South*, 1836; *Letters to Catherine Beecher*, 1838, http://utc.iath.virginia.edu/abolitn/grimkehp.html.

# Index

Page numbers in **boldface** are illustrations. Entries in **boldface** are glossary terms.

# About the Author

**SUSAN DUDLEY GOLD** is a writer, historian, editor, and graphic designer. Before becoming a children's book author, she worked as a newspaper reporter and magazine editor. She has written more than fifty books for middle- and high-school students on a wide range of topics. Her book on slavery and human rights, *United States v. Amistad: Slave Ship Mutiny* (Supreme Court Milestones), received a Carter G. Woodson Honor Book award. She has also written about slavery and civil rights in the books *Missouri Compromise* (Landmark Legislation), *Civil Rights Act of 1964* (Landmark Legislation), and *Brown v. Board of Education: Separate but Equal?* (Supreme Court Milestones). After serving a year as a VISTA volunteer, she currently manages a program to aid veterans. She and her husband live in Maine, where they own a web design and publishing company.